A CONVERSATION
WITH JESUS

ON

HOPE

A CONVERSATION
WITH JESUS

ON

HOPE

DAVID HELM

CHRISTIAN
FOCUS

Scripture quotations are from *The Holy Bible, English Standard Version*, copyright © 2001 by Crossway Bibles, a publishing ministry of Good News Publishers. Used by permission. All rights reserved. ESV Text Edition: 2011.

Copyright © Holy Trinity Church, Chicago

ISBN 978-1-5271-0329-0

Published in 2019

by

Christian Focus Publications Ltd.,
Geanies House, Fearn, Ross-shire,
IV20 1TW, Great Britain

www.christianfocus.com

Cover design and typeset by: Pete Barnsley (CreativeHoot.com)

Printed in China

CONTENTS

TWO WORDS
BEFORE
BEGINNING

ONE

The book in your hands is one of six. Short volumes all. Think of them as people to meet, not pages to be read. In each, a charcoal sketch is drawn of a person who first appeared on the pages of John's Gospel. Both women and men. Real flesh and blood. All worthy of attention. And each one fully capable of standing on their own two feet.

Beyond this, they all have someone in common. Jesus. The Nazarene. The Christ—he who forever changed the world we live in. Anyway, they all met him. In person. And they talked with him. More than that. Each one had a *conversation with Jesus* about something important to them.

TWO

I suppose something should be said about why 'these six'? Let's just say the selection is subjective. Author's prerogative. I liked them. I wanted to know them. And I learned significant things from each one of them. There are good reasons to think that you will connect with them too. Their struggles are our struggles. Their questions too. In fact, some people are saying there has never been another century to resemble the one these six lived in, until ours came along. And if that is the case, you may just run into yourself by running into them.

At any rate, there came a day when they all ran into Jesus. Of course, he is the only character to emerge in every encounter. I am confident that you will enjoy getting to know him.

DIRECTOR'S
NOTES

CAST:

🌿 **MARY:** a woman, shattered, with rumpled clothing and in mourning

🌿 **JESUS:** a young man, animated, dressed like an ordinary gardener

🌿 **ANGELS:** two of them, messengers in human likeness

SETTING:

A cemetery set upon a rolling landscape. Just before dawn. The stonewalled city of Jerusalem is in the near distance, awaiting the coming warmth of sunrise. But here, cave-like tombs are present, having been cut into the hillside.

The woman, careful in step, follows what little light the night sky affords up a small gravel path toward a cave. Not until drawing near is she alarmed. The great stone entrance has been pushed aside and light is escaping from inside.

A CONVERSATION WITH JESUS ON
HOPE

My love and my fortune,
'Tis an evil portion
To lay for a giant,
A shroud and a coffin;

…

Oh, rider of the bright eyes
What happened you yesterday?
I thought you in my heart
When I bought you your fine clothes
One the world could not slay….

—FROM AN ANCIENT IRISH ELEGY[1]

Death destroys hope. The finality of it all. A life lost. A loved one's companionship concluded. And beyond death? Beyond this? A resurrection on the last day? The everlasting kingdom of God? Is it even possible? Is there reason for such a hope?

In 1950, Par Lagerkvist published the novel *Barabbas*. His chapters covering the nights between Jesus' death and resurrection are especially captivating. Ironically, it isn't Barabbas, but a young girl who becomes the central figure. She had met Jesus once. He had filled her life with hope, even hope in a resurrection from the dead and entrance into God's eternal kingdom. Lagerkvist imagines her now, in the pre-dawn stillness of the third day, alone, near the cemetery and waiting for Jesus' resurrection:

> *She lay looking up at the stars and thought of what was soon to come... No, she did not want to fall asleep, she wanted to keep watch this night... Tomorrow at sunrise... Tomorrow at sunrise... It was almost beyond belief.*
>
> *She was glad she had been told about it... was not the night nearly over? Yes, the stars above her were no longer the same, and the crescent moon had long*

since gone down behind the hills… Yes, the night must now be over.

Now the morning star was rising over the Mount of Olives. She recognized it at once… she got up swiftly and hurried away into the darkness.[2]

I'm sure you can envision where she hurried off to. To the garden and the tomb. What were the words Lagerkvist used to describe her hope? 'Tomorrow at sunrise… Tomorrow at sunrise… It was almost beyond belief.'

That's it. '*Almost* beyond belief.' She hadn't given up. A smoking ember of residual hope for resurrection remained.

BEYOND HOPE

In the Biblical record, the word *almost* doesn't appear. For Jesus' followers at least, hopes for a resurrection had been snuffed out on the day Jesus died. His supporters were all, in total, simply *beyond* hope. A belief in the resurrection was unthinkable. Death brought complete devastation. It was just too much.

Perhaps you know the feeling?

In the Gospel of John, we are introduced to a woman overcome by the reality of death. Jesus' death. We meet her in the cemetery on that third day after Jesus has been executed.[3] Her name is Mary Magdalene. And, as John indicates, she wasn't anticipating a resurrection. Death had robbed her of that. Yet, in time, as we will see, this too would change. The aim here in this volume is to show us what made the change, what gave her renewed faith, and how her discovery can provide hope for us in a day of loss. As we look at the conversation Mary is going to have with a resurrected Jesus, you and I will have the opportunity to come to grips with death, and decide for ourselves whether or not it is reasonable to have hope of anything beyond this life. Mary is put before us in this way:

Now on the first day of the week Mary Magdalene came to the tomb early, while it was still dark, and saw that the stone had been taken away from the tomb. So she ran and went to Simon Peter and the other disciple, the one whom Jesus loved, and said to them, 'They have taken the Lord out of the tomb, and we do not know where they have laid him.'

From our perspective, living as removed as we do from the origins of the Christian faith, it comes as a surprise to learn that Mary didn't run to her friends announcing: 'Christ is risen! Christ is risen!' And they didn't reply in antiphonal voice: 'He is risen indeed!' Apparently, it all went down another way. We are told that when she first came upon the empty tomb she thought certain religious officials, or even the keeper of the cemetery perhaps, had put Jesus elsewhere. And if we had been the ones she came running to with her announcement, we would have taken her words to mean: 'Hey, something terrible has happened! Somebody has desecrated the tomb and moved Jesus' body without telling us.'

I suppose we are so accustomed to the Easter story, the hope of a real bodily resurrection, that we have been lulled into thinking the early followers of Jesus were expecting it. But no, it was not like that. And this is the very point we are trying to take in. Mary Magdalene, the one who would first see the resurrected Christ, entered the cemetery that day, well before dawn, in mourning. Death had won. Hope had died. Resurrection was the furthest thing from her mind.

In one sense, I am glad the Bible doesn't portray her like the young girl in Lagerkvist's novel. Mary Magdalene's likeness is more realistic. In fact, if the resurrection did occur (something you will have to make your own mind up on), this is the way it must have been. A complete surprise. After all, any ordinary person could not possibly have had any idea of what was about to happen, no matter how often Jesus may have spoken about it. A real resurrection from the dead is simply too astounding. Yes, from Mary's perspective there would be no resurrection. Jesus was gone and not coming back.

HOPE'S BURDEN OF PROOF

That said, Mary Magdalene did come back. The Gospel account makes that clear. She made a return visit to the tomb later that same morning. In all likelihood, she revisited only a short time after telling Peter and the others that she found the tomb empty. By now, of course, darkness was giving way, and the sun was on the rise. And we read: 'But Mary stood weeping outside the tomb.'

She wept for good reason. From what we can surmise from other accounts of her interactions with him, Jesus was someone who mattered a lot to her. She had suffered from severe spiritual oppression and, as a result, ostracization from the community. In healing her, Jesus took her off the garbage heap of life, put her in her right mind, and had given her a renewed sense of hope.

But on this day, she must have been doubly distraught. Not only had Jesus died, but his body had been moved. She no longer even knew where to go to mourn him. And so, we find her weeping. Many people today, perhaps even you, can identify with this. Belief fails. Hope dies. Something, or someone, has been taken. And we don't know where to go or how to get there. Suddenly, we are adrift. Any earlier assurance we have had that God was doing something wonderful in the world is shaken. Doubts arise. Despair emerges. We are left standing beside Mary Magdalene in grief.

It is during times like this that we wonder, what would it take for her—for any of us—to recover hope? What would convince us that God is still in control and working his purposes out? As Mary Magdalene stood outside the tomb that morning, with tears streaming down her face, only one answer would suffice. Jesus would need to rise from the dead. She would not settle for an imaginary Jesus or a mythical one. She could not. Like us, she is too sensible, too rooted to rebuild her life on naïveté—the blind notion that hope springs eternal. Jesus, in the flesh, would have to come back.

Resurrection. This is hope's burden of proof.

I have come to think that this is only right. For without a *real* resurrection, who can say in good faith that God accomplished something extraordinary in the world? Who can claim that God has done something strong enough to overcome our hopelessness, brought on by human frailty, sin, disease and especially death?

We must all face the facts. The burden of proof lies with the resurrection of Jesus. Without that, having faith in him is pointless. On this point, the poet John Updike had it right:

> *Make no mistake: if he rose at all*
> *It was as His body;*
> *If the cells' dissolution did not reverse,*
> *the molecules reknit, the amino acids rekindle,*
> *the Church will fall.*
>
> *It was not as the flowers,*
> *each soft Spring recurrent;*
> *it was not as His Spirit in the mouths and*
> *fuddled eyes of the eleven apostles;*
> *it was as His flesh: ours.*
>
> *The same hinged thumbs and toes,*
> *the same valued heart*
> *that—pierced—died, withered, paused, and*
> *then regathered out of enduring Might*
> *new strength to enclose.*
>
> *Let us not mock God with metaphor,*
> *analogy, sidestepping, transcendence,*
> *making of the event a parable, a sign painted*

in the faded credulity of earlier ages:
let us walk through the door.[4]

It is one thing to want the story of Christ's resurrection to be true. It is quite another for it to be true. Real hope must be fixed to the *real thing*.

This need for the real thing, a real resurrection, cannot be easily dumbed down to something less, at least not if it aims to hold people over time. Back in the 20th century, a movement took hold for a while in some Christian circles. It was championed by a few particular theologians who had disproportionate influence upon denominations (various groups within Protestantism).

The idea was this: In an effort to remain relevant (given that many no longer believed in miracles, let alone one as large as the resurrection), these theologians attempted to hold to the *spirit* of the thing. The hope of the resurrection became *symbolic*, something anyone could participate in, even if it never really happened. It was never much more than blind optimism, really. A cup of spiritual caffeine to get you through. Suffice it to say, the movement didn't last. Those churches are now empty, and their denominations are flagging. Why? With such a view, it only took a generation or two for people to realize that if that was all there was to the Christian message, they didn't really need it. They moved on.

Fortunately, we live now, and not then. And most of us have awakened to the fact that because death is real, and our grief is great, only a real resurrection provides us a chance of lasting hope. But for that, we will need to be made ready. Prepared even, before we can consider it as being true.

PREPARATION FOR HOPE

Helpfully, even before Mary has her conversation with Jesus, the Gospel of John records that she was made ready to believe that the *real thing* had happened. In other words, an event occurred to prepare her for the fact of a hope reborn. What was it that readied her? And can we learn anything from it that might assist us to experience the same?

Simply this. As she stood weeping outside the tomb, she did something—something significant—something that, by way of analogy, each one of us needs to do. The Bible says that she 'stooped to look in the tomb.' She walked through the door. This is an important detail. She stepped into the empty tomb to take a look for herself. She went in. And by way of metaphor, so must you. I don't know what has taken your hope. A relationship that died? A body that lies diseased? Even death? To continue to stand weeping over the shock of death is natural, even right. But in that same horrible moment, to decide to push through the tears and stoop under the lintel of possibility, well, that takes courage. A daring act of faith. I want to encourage you to take that same step. To consider, at least for the time it takes to read this short book, the empty tomb. Follow Mary Magdalene inside to see if there can possibly be anything more. As she looked in, she encountered a surprise, something astonishing which would make her ready for a conversation with a resurrected Jesus. We read:

> *And she saw two angels in white sitting where the body of Jesus had lain, one at the head and one at the feet. They said to her, 'Woman why are you weeping?' She said to them, 'They have taken away my Lord, and I do not know where they have laid him.'*

The Gospel writer strikingly mentions the presence of two angels. There they sit, like sparkling cherubim, at either end of the stone slab on which the body once lay (in the Old Testament, angelic creatures adorned the ark of the covenant, also one on either end, looking down upon the mercy seat, the place of blood sacrifice for our sins). What in the world are we to make of these two angels? Simply this, they were sent to prepare Mary Magdalene for an encounter with the risen Lord.

Let me explain. In the Bible, angels (or *messengers*—the same word is used for both) often make an appearance to interpret the activity of God in the world. In other words, they are created beings employed by God to help people make sense of what they would not ordinarily understand. Thus, when Jesus is born in Bethlehem, it is angels who appear to shepherds to announce to them what is really going on. Something just like that is happening here. Mary is getting a newsflash, a message of sorts, and in this instance, by way of a question, God is confronting her understanding of what has occurred. The two angels query her about weeping. As though they find her weeping an inappropriate response to the significance of an empty tomb. That is the extent of their words. In essence, they challenge her interpretation of things. And by doing so, they prepare her for something entirely unexpected: hope renewed.

That said, I don't tend to think that God is obliged to send you or me an angel, a messenger, to prepare us for a recovery of hope. The truth is, he doesn't need to. The Bible, the full and complete revelation of God to humanity, has been given to us in a way it was never given to Mary. We already possess his message, his revelation, his surprise announcement on what he is doing in the world. Given this fact, we should think that, like Mary, we are being prepared for an encounter with Christ simply as a result of reading his Word.

LIVING HOPE

Having been primed for the possibility of something greater, that is, having stooped into the tomb to take a look at things for herself, and having endured angelic questioning about weeping as her response to an empty tomb, Mary is as ready as she will ever be to have her own conversation with Jesus. I say, 'as ready as she will ever be,' knowing that one can never be fully prepared for a thing like that! And yet, what transpires next, her conversation with Jesus, will forever restore the hope she had at first. May it do the same for many of us. The start of her conversation with Jesus went like this:

> Having said this, she turned around and saw Jesus standing, but she did not know that it was Jesus. Jesus said to her, 'Woman why are you weeping? Whom are you seeking?' Supposing him to be the gardener, she said to him, 'Sir, if you have carried him away, tell me where you have laid him, and I will take him away.'

Jesus opened with a question, the same question the angels had just asked her seconds before: 'Woman why are you weeping?' But here, he adds a second one to it: 'Whom are you seeking?' When the two questions are put together, they appear to express an attitude of wanting to help, to assist in some way. To paraphrase them, it is as though he is asking: 'Woman, what is it that makes you this sad? And who is it that you wish to see?' Put differently: 'What caused your sorrow, and who can I help you to find?'

If this is the case, and I think it is, these opening words also express knowledge. They convey a tone of real compassion. They reveal a sense that he could actually assist her. In essence, they are the words of a man who appears to know how to remedy her pain. We know she took the words this way, for when she responded to him, she did so, 'supposing him to be the gardener.' In other words, she thought he might be aware, given his assumed vocation and presence in the cemetery, of where the body had been taken. All the while, Mary was completely unaware!

She had just spoken to the very one she had been seeking.

The fact that she thought Jesus was the cemetery gardener (arriving for his morning shift) is perfect! She didn't recognize Jesus at first. She saw him, but she didn't know that it was him. To my way of thinking, this detail adds credibility to the account. After all, fabricated accounts are far more likely to omit details which expose the central figures to embarrassment.

The complete irony of this scene amuses. We are meant to envisage Mary Magdalene, tearfully standing just inside the entrance of the tomb, having just spoken with angels who asked her why she is weeping. And now, turning, only seconds later, she is looking back out into the cemetery grounds. There she sees a man framed in the doorway whom she supposes to be the gardener, who asks her the exact same question. This man though, obviously animated, is standing in the light, while she remains fixed in the dark.

Humorous? Yes. But her responses to Jesus' questions ring true to our own experience in loss. When we endure the death of a loved one, sorrow can easily blind us. We cannot see the comfort of the resurrection. Our eyes remain captive to lament and we can't seem to find the one we are seeking.

If the resurrection of Jesus is true though, some measure of comfort is possible. In fact, Jesus anticipated this need even before his death. Earlier in the Gospel of John, he said to his followers:

> *Let not your hearts be troubled. Believe in God; believe also in me. In my Father's house are many rooms. If it were not so, would I have told you that I go to prepare a place for you? And if I go and prepare a place for you, I will come again and will take you to myself, that where I am you may be also.*[5]

Remember this, if the resurrection is true, comfort in sorrow is attainable. Hope is available. But how?

RESURRECTION HOPE RECOGNIZED

We should pay close attention to the next words in their conversation, for by them we will know what it was that changed Mary Magdalene's outlook, how it happened, and grasp the hope that can be ours in an hour of loss.

Mary Magdalene's return to life-changing belief did not come by seeing Jesus. After all, we have already observed that she had seen him without knowing that it was him. Instead, as we will see, her hope was restored in recognizing his voice. And this singular truth, that faith comes by hearing a word, has life-restoring power when we are lost in a sea of sorrows. Take a look at how her conversation with Jesus went, how her recovery of hope happened:

Jesus said to her, 'Mary.' She turned and said to him in Aramaic, 'Rabboni!' (which means Teacher). Jesus said to her, 'Do not cling to me, for I have not yet ascended to the Father; but go to my brothers and say to them, "I am ascending to my Father and your Father, to my God and your God."'

Did you catch it? How recognition came? Jesus called her by name. 'Mary.' That was it. In that, her hope was reborn. Amazing. It is by hearing, not seeing, that Mary knew Jesus and grasped that he had been raised from the dead! Sight gave way to the supremacy of sound. It was a *word* that made her complete. And because she hears him, she now sees him and calls out to him and runs to him and hugs him and becomes a lifelong believer in him.

By a word received, she soars above her sorrows.

As for Jesus, he indicates to her that he is about to ascend back to the Father. His work on earth is done. Death is defeated. Hope is reborn. Access to heaven is hers.

That is all well and good for Mary. But what about us? How do we grab hold of the same hope Mary grasped? After all, Jesus is not here, but in heaven.

THE POWER OF A WORD

These are important questions. And the answer should encourage. Let me explain: It surprises us to learn that Mary's faith in Christ, and her hope in the resurrection, comes by hearing the word of Jesus. It did not come at first by having her own personal encounter in seeing Jesus. It came by a word. And in light of this, what are we to make of it? Of the power of a *word*?

Many people have trouble believing in the Christian message and the notion of the hope of the resurrection because they weren't there to see it for themselves. 'Wasn't Mary

Magdalene given an unfair advantage over us? Didn't she see Jesus with her own eyes? Wasn't she given face-to-face time to evaluate Jesus and his message? What hope is there for any of us to get such direct contact with a risen Christ?' Such questions deserve a thoughtful response. To put the issue directly: Are there good reasons for you to make a fresh start with Jesus Christ, even though you were not alive to witness his resurrection for yourself? (see *A Conversation with Jesus on Doubt* in this series for more on this).

Evidently, we are not as disadvantaged as we think we are. The writer of this Gospel held a deep conviction that people not only would or could come to a reasonable belief in Jesus as a result of the *words* (long after the first century), but should. Shortly after narrating the conversation Mary had with Jesus, we read:

> *Now Jesus did many other signs in the presence of his disciples, which are*

not written in this book; but these are written so that you may believe that Jesus is the Christ, the Son of God, and that by believing you may have life in his name.

The Gospel account could not have answered our questions any more directly. Not only did John anticipate that many will believe, and thereby have hope restored and the prospect of eternal life before them, but he went so far as to show us that is possible. You and I can have hope. We can arrive at a fresh and restored belief simply on the basis of what we read and hear. To put it succinctly, you and I can come to faith in Jesus Christ and the hope of the resurrection through reading and listening to God's Word. Is it any wonder then that Christians give themselves to Bible reading, and especially so in times of loss? For when God's Word is read, his voice is heard and our hope is reborn.

THE IMPORTANCE OF THE RESURRECTION

At this point we must take leave of Mary Magdalene for a moment. The Gospel writers and the rest of the New Testament are united in their view that if the bodily resurrection of Jesus truly occurred, then everything changes for them. Today, however, you might be thinking, 'How so? Why? What is it that actually changes? What is the real and ongoing significance of Jesus' resurrection? How does it help me with the sorrow of death?'

For answers to these questions, you need to have a basic handle on the message of the Bible. The resurrection is essential to God's eternal plans for us as set forth at creation. He created us to be in relationship with him—to live with him—forever. But we sinned. All of us. Therefore, we are subjected to death, the just penalty for going our own way. To have our hope restored, we would need someone to pay the penalty for sin, someone who would not be held captive to its power. In essence, we need a Savior and a King! One who would suffer on our behalf, yet is strong enough to overcome our biggest enemy: death.

Think of it this way: Without the resurrection of Jesus from the dead, God's purposes for us in creation remain unmet. Our problem continues unresolved. And God's promises go unfulfilled. But with the resurrection of Jesus, we have assurance that our problem has been resolved. Death has been overcome and peace with God has been made. And that is what gives us hope!

RESURRECTION HOPE AND YOU

So, what are we to do with all that we have read? Has it provided us with a reason for hope? Even in the midst of all that you have lost? Our individual histories are littered with experiences and losses that have robbed us of hope: abuses endured in childhood, handicaps affecting our appearance and ability to move, dark clouds of depression that never seem to lift, difficult living conditions, economic deprivation, bias, hardship, incarceration, relational strife, sickness and disease, and that final enemy, death. So where do we turn from here?

Let me see if I can help. At the outset, Mary Magdalene served as our central figure. Yet, as we conclude, it is the resurrected Jesus who occupies us most. Early on we identified with Mary, but now we must decide to identify with Jesus. Of course, what you end up making of his resurrection from the dead will be the deciding issue. And on this point, I have tried to be clear. A discovery of belief, or a recovery of hope for something beyond death, hinges entirely on the veracity of the resurrection. It must be real and not imagined. Resurrection must be as real as death.

Are you prepared to make a fresh start with God? Has life, and death, and the loss of hope brought you to a place where a recovery of belief is needed? Or, perhaps, are you beginning to understand the importance of belief for the very first time? Yes, we all need hope. We all need God to step into our lives. We all need to emerge from the darkness of the tomb we are in.

But don't get me wrong. Don't confuse hope with happiness. Taking up with Jesus won't magically take away the pain you feel. Coming to faith in Christ is not about escaping difficult circumstances in life. It is about coming to that which is true for your eternal sake.

Yes. If we have learned anything from this vignette of Mary Magdalene, we have learned that we need Jesus for more than a change of circumstance. We need Jesus for life. We will need Jesus in death. We need Jesus in payment of our sins. And we need Jesus for the hope of our own resurrection. If you resonate with these truths, the hope of the gospel can be yours. You simply need to place your trust in Jesus.

I want to invite you to a better hope by embracing the words of the gospel about Jesus.

🌱 He died for our sins and was raised from the dead on the third day in accordance with the promises made about him in the Bible.

🌱 His resurrection shows that death is defeated and hope for a right relationship with God is available to all who repent of their sin and turn to him.

🌱 Those who put their faith in him are born again into a hope better than anything this world has to offer.

🌱 His death and resurrection are our only source of comfort and hope in this life and the next.

If you believe these things are true, then you have a reason for hope.

Finally, the story of Mary Magdalene ends by telling us what she did after her faith in Christ was secure. It reads:

> *Mary Magdalene went and announced to the disciples, 'I have seen the Lord'— and that he had said these things to her.*

What a different person Mary is now! She is setting out *from* the tomb. She had come in the darkness, with her pace slow, her heart heavy, and her hope lost. But now, she leaves in the light. Her steps are quick, her heart is hopeful, and her own voice can be heard. 'It's true. It really is. Despair will not last. Death will not… it cannot win. No. Jesus won the victory! He overcame death. And in him, all things will one day be new.'

How great it would be if what happened to her is now happening to you! If you have placed your faith in Christ as a result of reading this short book, I want to encourage you to do the same thing Mary did. Go and tell a Christian friend that you too have seen the Lord, that you have hope of your faith being restored, and that Jesus has revealed himself to you by the Bible's very own words.

Once you do that, it would also be good to seek out a church that believes these things. That kind of church can help you grow.

JOHN 20:1-18

¹ Now on the first day of the week Mary Magdalene came to the tomb early, while it was still dark, and saw that the stone had been taken away from the tomb. ² So she ran and went to Simon Peter and the other disciple, the one whom Jesus loved, and said to them, 'They have taken the Lord out of the tomb, and we do not know where they have laid him.' ³ So Peter went out with the other disciple, and they were going toward the tomb. ⁴ Both of them were running together, but the other disciple outran Peter and reached the tomb first. ⁵ And stooping to look in, he saw the linen cloths lying there, but he did not go in. ⁶ Then Simon Peter came, following him, and went into the tomb. He saw the linen cloths lying there, ⁷ and the face cloth, which had been on Jesus' head, not lying with the linen cloths but folded up in a place by itself. ⁸ Then the other disciple, who had reached the tomb first, also went in, and he saw and believed; ⁹ for as yet they did not understand the Scripture, that he must rise from the dead. ¹⁰ Then the disciples went back to their homes. ¹¹ But Mary stood weeping outside the tomb, and as she wept she stooped to look into the tomb. ¹² And she saw two angels in white, sitting where the body of Jesus had lain, one at the head and one at the feet. ¹³ They said to her, 'Woman, why are you weeping?' She said to them, 'They have taken away my Lord, and I do not know where they have laid him.' ¹⁴ Having said this, she turned around and saw Jesus standing, but she did not know that it was Jesus. ¹⁵ Jesus said to her, 'Woman, why are you weeping? Whom are you seeking?' Supposing him to be the gardener, she said to him, 'Sir, if you have carried him away, tell me where you have laid him, and I will take him away.' ¹⁶ Jesus said to her, 'Mary.' She turned and said to him in Aramaic, 'Rabboni!' (which means Teacher). ¹⁷ Jesus said to her, 'Do not cling to me, for I have not yet ascended to the Father; but go to my brothers and say to them, "I am ascending to my Father and your Father, to my God and your God."' ¹⁸ Mary Magdalene went and announced to the disciples, 'I have seen the Lord'—and that he had said these things to her.

ENDNOTES

1. Ed. Susan Cahill, *For the Love of Ireland*, (New York: Balantine Books, 2001), 217-219.

2. Par Lagerkvist, *Barabbas*, (New York: Vintage Books, 1951), 32-41.

3. This woman's encounter with Jesus can be found in full by reading the John 20:1-18. I encourage you to read it. The text can be found on pages 49-50. Unless otherwise marked, all subsequent quotations are from this passage.

4. John Updike, 'Seven Stanzas at Easter' in *Selected Poems*, (New York: Penguin, 2015), 15.

5. John 14: 1-3.

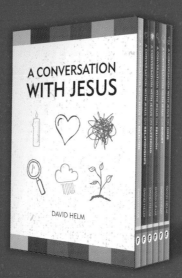

A CONVERSATION WITH JESUS ON RELIGION

Nicodemus was a religious man. He knew the religious law inside out and made sure he kept to it—he even taught it to others. He was confident that his religion would save him; after all, he was a good person.

But then he met Jesus.

According to Jesus his best attempts at living the moral life wouldn't save him. But if religion won't make us right with God, what will? Jesus gave Nicodemus an answer, but what does it mean?

9781527103245

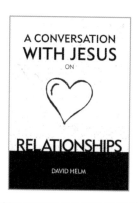

A CONVERSATION WITH JESUS
ON RELATIONSHIPS

She wasn't particularly spiritual. She was looking for something else. A series of failed relationships behind her, she kept hoping for a real connection. Something that would last forever. Something that would satisfy that desire within her.

And then she met Jesus.

Her trip to get water from the well turns into a discussion about living water—and a relationship with the living God. A relationship better than all her previous relationships, that will endure, and give her the satisfaction she has been seeking.

9781527103252

A CONVERSATION WITH JESUS
ON SUFFERING

He had been subject to a protracted and excruciating
life of suffering. He was well aware of the unrelenting
persistence of human misery. If anyone had a reason to
feel betrayed by God, this man did.

But then he met Jesus.

At Jesus' command, this man who hasn't walked for 38
years is suddenly on his feet. But this healing brings many
questions. Why this man and not another? Why was he
suffering in the first place? And what would this man do
now he could walk?

9781527103269

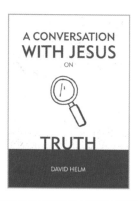

A CONVERSATION WITH JESUS ON TRUTH

What is truth? This question, asked by Pilate, a Roman governor in Jerusalem, has echoed down through the centuries and still has ramifications today. His job as representative of Rome and Roman law required that he discover the truth about the charges brought against the prisoner before him.

So he asked Jesus.

The answer Jesus gives and Pilate's reaction are enlightening. The truthfulness of Jesus' words matter. Will you respond in the same way as Pilate?

9781527103276

A CONVERSATION WITH JESUS
ON DOUBT

Doubt is a virtue—a necessary check on blind certainty. 'Doubting Thomas' is a man who has been known for his doubt throughout history. He was one of Jesus' early followers and he was a man who liked to make up his own mind based on the evidence available to him. When the other disciples told him they'd seen Jesus alive again it sounded outrageous.

But then he saw Jesus.

The evidence of his own eyes, ears, and hands, backed up what his fellow disciples had been saying. But Jesus had a thing or two to say about Thomas' doubt.

9781527103283

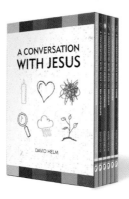

A CONVERSATION WITH JESUS BOXSET

This box contains six short volumes. Six people to meet. Each appeared on the pages of John's Gospel. Each met Jesus—the Nazarene, the Christ, the man who forever changed the world we live in. And each had a conversation with Jesus about something important to them. Through these conversations you can meet not only these six men and women, but the man who changed everything too.

9781527103238